Marvelous Marbles

by Beth Dvergsten Stevens

D1738378

Perfection Learning® CA

Cover Illustration: Mike Aspengren
Inside Illustration: Mike Aspengren

Dedication

For my family and marble lovers everywhere. With special
thanks to Norm M. for his input.

About the Author

Beth Stevens is a writer and former teacher. She currently
writes stories and develops crafts and games for children's
magazines. She also writes a weekly newspaper column for
kids. Her first book, *Celebrate Christmas Around the World*,
was a teacher's resource book.

Although she's no longer in the classroom, she still loves
teaching and learning. She hopes her readers will discover
something new and interesting every time they open one of
her books! Beth lives in Waverly, Iowa, with her husband, three
children, and their pets.

Perfection Learning® Corporation,
1000 North Second Avenue,
P.O. Box 500, Logan, Iowa 51546-1099.
Phone: 1-800-831-4190 • Fax: 1-712-644-2392

Paperback 0-7891-2872-1
Cover Craft® 0-7807-7834-0

Contents

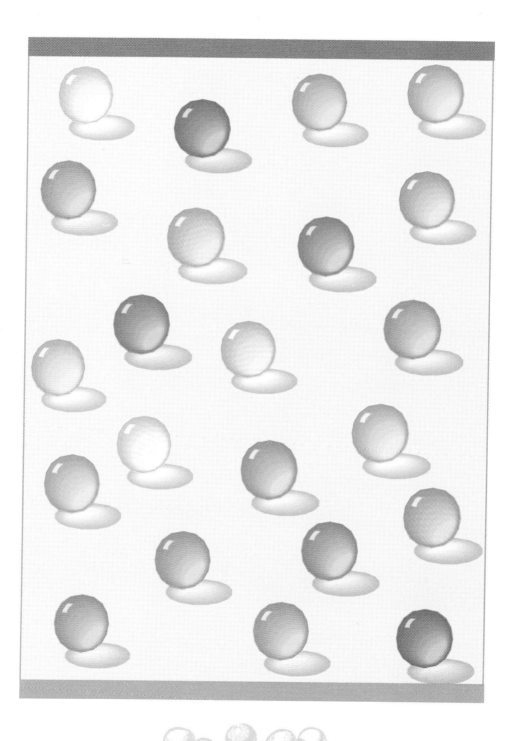

4

Chapter 1

History of Marbles in the World

Balls of clay. Nuts. Small stones. Fruit pits. How are these things alike?

They are all round. They are found in nature. And children played games with them. These were the first toy marbles.

Long ago, children didn't have fancy toys. But they did have marbles.

Children made their own marbles. They used anything that was small and round.

Some children even used small stones.

Other children used fruit seeds. Some even used nuts. And some children rolled soft clay into balls.

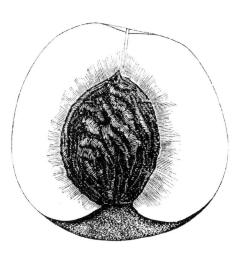

These children made up marble games. And they played these games for hours.

The first marble game was played by men in Greece. It was played almost 3,000 years ago.

In one very old story about the Odyssey, the writer tells about a marble game. Many men wanted to marry the same woman. So they played a game of marbles.

One man won. He became the husband.

Luckily, husbands aren't chosen that way today!

Over 2,000 years ago, children in the Old World played with marbles too. Their marbles were made of stone. Old marbles have also been found in Africa and Central America.

Time passed. Many more people learned to play marble games. They shared their games with people they met.

By the 1400s, marbles were common in Europe. Children played many fun games.

Some families from Europe crossed the ocean on ships. They came to live in the New World.

The children brought their marbles. They thought no one else in the world played with marbles. But they were wrong!

The New World already had marbles! Native Americans had clay and stone ones. They knew lots of marble games too. In fact, some Indians had been playing marbles for 1,500 years or more!

So you see, marbles are very old toys. Children and adults everywhere have played with them. And they are still popular. Can you think of other toys or games that are this old?

Chapter 2

History of Marbles in America

More and more families came to America. Marbles came with them. Marble games were popular.

Many marbles came from Germany. Some were made from **porcelain.** Some were

onyx

made from **semiprecious stones.** Some of

agate

these stones were onyx, tiger's-eye, marble, and agate.

Marbles made from agate were called **aggies.** Large pieces of the stone were chipped into small cubes. The chips were smoothed into beautiful balls.

Sometimes the stones were smoothed by hand. This was done on a grinding stone.

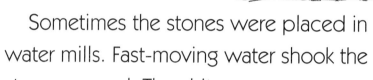

Sometimes the stones were placed in water mills. Fast-moving water shook the stones around. They hit against one another. This made the sharp edges round and smooth.

Children loved aggies. Bands of color ran through the stone. But they cost a lot to make.

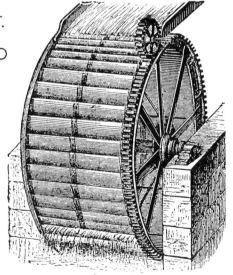

So they cost a lot to buy. Not every child could own them. Aggies are valued by marble collectors today.

After a while, people made marbles from  other things. Pottery and china factories made marbles from clay. They baked the marbles in hot ovens. Lots of pottery marbles were brown with a blue **glaze.** Many of these were called **Benningtons.**

China marbles were made from fine white clay. These marbles were painted by hand. Some had pretty designs.

Clay marbles weren't as strong as stone marbles. But they cost less. More children could buy them.

Some glass factories made glass marbles.

These marbles had colored bands in the
middle. Children loved them. They were
very pretty. And they cost less than stone
marbles. Soon toy-makers were making glass
marbles too.

By 1906, new machines were invented. These machines made marbles quickly.

Marble factories in Ohio made a million marbles a day! German factories still made stone and glass marbles by hand. But in 1926, Germany started using machines.

Some factories made marbles from other things. They made hollow steel marbles called **steelies.** Other factories made wooden marbles.

Most steel and wooden marbles were not good for games. They were not the right weight. Sometimes steelies broke the other marbles!

In the 1950s, Japanese factories made many glass marbles. One type was called **cat's-eye.** The cat's-eye became popular in the United States. These marbles didn't cost a lot.

Cat's-eyes were interesting to look at. They were clear glass with a band of color in the middle. They looked like the eye of a cat! You have probably seen lots of these.

Marbles come in different sizes. The smallest marbles are called **pee wees**. They are $\frac{1}{2}$ inch or less across. The largest marbles can be 2 to 3 inches across!

A **game marble** is the most common size. It's a little smaller than a dime.

Game marbles were sometimes called **mibs** or **commies.** Mibs were stone marbles. Commies were common clay marbles.

Most marble players had lots of game marbles. They also had some special marbles that were bigger. The bigger marbles were called **shooters** or **taws.** Shooters are about 1 inch across.

Where did children keep all their marbles? They kept them in small leather bags. Boys collected the most marbles. But many girls collected marbles too. This was especially true if they had older brothers.

Sometimes children traded marbles. They traded to get different ones for their collections. Children still trade things. Have you ever traded sports cards, stickers, or pogs?

Today you can buy glass marbles in stores. They don't cost very much. And they are very colorful!

Many new marbles are made in Mexico and Japan. One company in Virginia still makes marbles.

Some artists make copies of old marbles. They even sign and date them!

Chapter 3

Playing with Marbles

There are different kinds of marble games. Some are still popular today. Some players even go to marble tournaments. They play Tournament Ringer. The best marble players win prizes!

Most marble games have a target. The target can be a line or a hole. Or it can be another player's marble.

Sometimes players roll their shooters to hit a game marble. Then the game marble moves toward the target. The player that gets the closest wins.

Be a Good Player

A good marble player is a good shooter. It is important to shoot the taw, or shooter, straight and hard. It takes lots of practice! Try it.

1. Cup your hand. Put your hand on the floor with the first two knuckles touching it. This is called "knuckling down."

2. Set a shooter between your first two fingers. Place your thumb behind the shooter. Hold your elbow up. Keep your knuckles down.

3. Take aim. Use your thumb to flick the shooter toward a game marble.

Did you hit the game marble? Did it roll? Where did your shooter go?

Does your shooter fly off in strange directions? You're flicking it too hard. Shoot easier. And try to add some back spin.

Keep practicing! You'll get it!

In the past, children played Ringer. One player drew a big circle in the dirt. Players put their game marbles inside the circle.

Players tried to knock each other's game marbles out of the ring with their shooters. The player who shot the most marbles out of the ring won.

Today you might not play marble games in the dirt. You might play on concrete or a wood floor. Then the marbles don't jump in odd ways!

And your ring can be a chalk line or a piece of yarn. You might use a tennis shoe as a target. You can also use a shoe box with holes cut in the sides.

Some marble games need special game boards. Solitaire is one example. You play this game alone.

Chinese Checkers is another example. It was invented in the late 1930s. It is still popular today.

Have you ever played these games? Marble games are fun! Try some today!

Chapter 4

Games to Try

When you play marbles, you can make up
your own rules. You can play inside or
outside. You can play in dirt or on carpet.
You can use special game boards. Or you
can make your own.

Getting Started

Who goes first in a marble game? There is a way to choose! It is called **lagging.**

Draw two lines. Leave 12 inches between them. Take ten big steps away from the lines. Draw another line here. This is the **pitching line.**

Each player stands behind the pitching line. Each tosses, or pitches, a marble at the first line. The player whose marble stops closest to the first line goes first. If a marble crosses the back line, that player goes last.

Now you're ready to try a few games.

Ringer

A favorite game

Needs

- two or more players
- game marbles—the same number for each player
- one shooter for each player
- chalk, yarn, or string to make a ring

Set up

Make a ring. It can be 1½ to 10 feet across. Each player puts four to six game marbles inside the ring.

Object of the game

Be the player to hit the most marbles out of the ring.

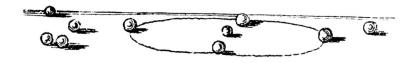

Play

- Shooters can be placed anywhere outside the ring.
- Players take turns. Each flicks a shooter into the ring.
- If a player doesn't knock out a marble, the turn is over.
- If some marbles and the shooter roll out, the turn ends. The marbles are placed back in the ring.
- If marbles roll out and the shooter stays in, the player takes those marbles. And another turn.

Ringer for Keeps

Play it the same as Ringer. But at the end of the game, you keep the marbles you hit out! Don't **play for keeps** with your special marbles!

Spanning Games

The bigger your hand is,
the easier it is to play!

Needs

- marbles
- more than one player

Set up

Practice spanning. Stretch out your open hand between two marbles. Try to touch both marbles. If you can, you have spanned it!

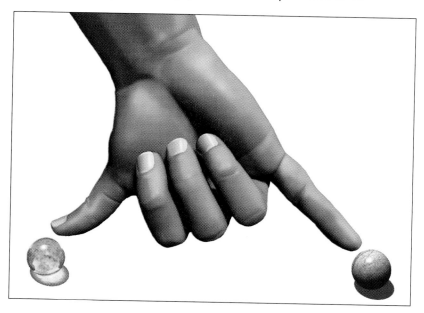

Object of the game

Hit or span the most marbles.

Play for Hit and Span, Bossout, and Going to School

- One player rolls a game marble any distance. This is a *jack*.
- The next player tries to roll a marble close to the jack.
- If the marble hits the jack or if the two can be spanned, the player keeps both marbles.
- If the jack is missed and the two marbles cannot be spanned, both marbles stay in place. The shooter's marble becomes the new jack.
- A player who hits or spans the new jack gets to keep all the marbles in play.

Target Games

Take good aim!

Needs

- a target. It can be a chalk line, holes in the ground, or a cardboard box.

Set up

Get your target ready.

Play for Stroke, Plum Pudding, or Picking Plums

- Draw two lines, 3 feet apart.
- Each player places the same number of marbles along one line. Place them 2 inches apart.
- Players kneel behind the other line.
- Players take turns. Each one flicks a shooter toward the line.
- Players keep any marbles they knock off the line.

Play using a shoe box

- Cut holes into the side of a shoe box.
- Write a number between 1 and 5 above each hole. Put larger numbers at the ends. Put smaller numbers in the middle.
- Draw a shooting line.
- Take turns flicking marbles toward the holes from behind a line.
- Marbles that don't roll into a hole must stay where they land.
- When a marble goes into a hole, the shooter takes the number of marbles written above the hole. For example, a marble goes into a hole numbered 4. The player then chooses four marbles lying outside the box.

Solitaire or Hig

A game to play by yourself!

Needs

- a special board with 33 holes
- 32 marbles a little larger than the holes on the board

Set up

Put a marble in every
hole except the middle one.

Object of the game

Leave only one marble on the board.

Play

Jump one marble over another into an
empty hole.
Remove every marble that is jumped.

Dropping Games

Good games for an uneven surface!

Needs

- several players
- a chalk or yarn circle
- a bunch of marbles

Set up

Make a big circle on the ground and put some marbles inside it.

Play for Bombers, Tearing up the Pea Patch, Nuts, or Dropsies

- Players stand up around the circle and take turns.
- Drop a marble from eyeball height. Try to hit the marbles inside the circle.
- If marbles are knocked out, the player takes them.
- If a dropped marble doesn't go out of the circle, it must stay inside.

Different Names for Marble Games

- China: **Ishihajiki** uses small pebbles.

- Japan: **Ohajiki** uses flat pieces of plastic or glass.

- Britain: **Ring Taw** is like Ringer with a pitching line.

- Scotland: **Carpet Bowling** uses big marbles. More than 3 inches wide! It was popular in the late 1800s.

Chapter 5

Make Marrididdles!

Take a step back in time! Make a set of clay marbles just like children did long ago. They called clay marbles **marrididdles.** Follow this recipe. It makes 25–40 marbles.

Clay

Needs

- 1 cup flour
- ¼ cup salt
- 6 tablespoons water

Steps

1. Ask an adult to help.
2. Turn oven to 250°.
3. Put the ingredients in a bowl. Mix with a spoon.
4. Knead with hands for five minutes. Or until smooth.
5. Break off small pieces. Roll into small hard balls. They should be about $\frac{1}{2}$ inch wide. Make at least one bigger ball for your shooter.
6. Put marbles on cookie sheet. Bake for $\frac{1}{2}$ hour. Then turn marbles over. Bake for $1\frac{1}{2}$ hours longer.
7. Paint with acrylic paint when cool. Or spray with clear varnish.

How to Decorate

- Leave your marbles white.
- Add food coloring to clay. Blue and brown were used long ago.
- Paint simple designs on marbles. Use a paintbrush and acrylic craft paint. Paint leaves, bull's-eyes, flowers, rings, coils, or turkey tracks. They'll look just like old china marbles!

Now try your marbles! Are they round enough to roll well? Why not make a game to go with your marbles!

Pigs in Clover Marble Maze

In 1889, a man invented a game called Pigs in Clover. Marbles were the pigs. Players had to get the pigs into the center pen.

The game was very popular! People played it for hours and hours. In fact, they didn't get much work done.

Follow these directions to make your own maze.

Needs

- compass
- a pizza box lid or heavy cardboard
- old cereal box
- scissors
- ruler
- table knife
- low temperature glue gun
- tape

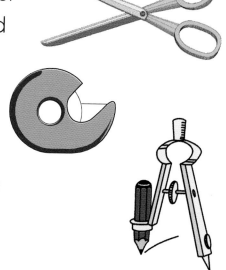

Steps

1. Make a 7-inch circle on the cardboard.
2. Draw another circle $\frac{7}{8}$ inch inside the first one.
3. Draw two more circles. Each $\frac{7}{8}$ inch inside the one before.
4. Press a table knife down along all the circles to make a dent.
5. Cut out the cardboard circle along outside line.
6. Cut four to five 1-inch wide strips from the cereal box.
7. Measure and cut strips to the following lengths.
   - strip 1: $4\frac{1}{2}$ inches long
   - strip 2: 10 inches long
   - strip 3: 15 inches long
   - strip 4: 22 inches long

   Tape strips together to make them long enough.
8. Roll the strips around your finger to bend them.

9. **Ask an adult to help with the gluing.** Put a line of glue along the inside circle. Leave a ¾-inch opening where ends don't meet. Place one long edge of strip 1 on glue. This will form a wall. Hold in place until glue is set.

10. On the next circle, mark a spot for the opening on the opposite side of first circle. Glue strip 2 in place with open edges at mark.

11. Glue on strip 3 in the same manner, with the opening on same side as the first circle.

12. Glue the last strip around outside of circle, overlapping ends. There should be no opening.

Play

Set a marble in the outer ring and move the board until the marble makes it to the small center ring. Now the pig is in the pen!

Chapter 6

Be a Marble Collector

Flea markets, auctions, and garage sales are great places to find old marbles! Check gardens, attics, and old buildings too.

People have dug up marbles in their gardens. Carpenters have found bags of marbles in old attics.

Workmen have found marbles inside old furnaces. Children probably dropped them through the heat vents.

People have even found marbles in old outhouses!

Look closely at the marbles you find. Are they perfectly round? Some marbles aren't. These marbles were probably made by hand. It was hard to make clay balls perfectly round.

Other handmade marbles were chipped from stone. Then they were smoothed on a grindstone. It was hard to make these perfectly round too.

They have many tiny flat spots. The flat spots are called *facets* or *faces.* If you look closely you may see these flat spots.

Handmade marbles are old and rare. Handmade stone marbles are especially valued!

But most marbles are perfectly round. Most marbles are made of glass. They were made by machines. The machines made many marbles at one time. All the marbles looked alike. Many have colored ribbons, swirls of bright colors, or shiny speckles in the middle.

But should you collect glass marbles? Yes! Glass marbles are fun to collect. And they're pretty! They're also easy to find. They don't cost very much. And some glass marbles are worth a lot of money!

The earliest machine-made marbles are very old. So they are valued by collectors.

Other machine-made marbles had mistakes. Maybe the colors were mixed wrong. And the workers didn't like how they looked.

Sometimes the first or last marbles from the machine didn't look like the others. These marbles are rare. There aren't very many of them. So these marbles are valuable.

Is It Glass or Stone?

- Are there bubbles inside a marble? If so, it is made from glass.
- Are there fine lines on a marble? If so, it's probably an old stone marble.
- Old agates might have small spots or tiny cracks inside. Even though the outside is perfect.

Children had things to go with their marbles. These were called **accessories.** These are prized by collectors too.

Accessories to collect

- leather or cloth marble bags
- boxes that held marble sets
- playing boards

Other marble things to collect

- coloring books
- photos
- magazines, books, and posters that show children playing marbles

Today, some marble collectors show off their best marbles in glass jars. Other collectors set them on a Solitaire game board. You might even catch them playing with those marbles!

Tips for Beginning Collectors

1. Look at lots and lots of marbles. Pay attention to the colors, swirls, and ribbons in the glass. How are they alike? How are they different?

2. Go to the library and look at marble books. Try to learn about different marbles.

3. Start by collecting cat's-eyes. Use marble books to learn which company made each one.

4. Collect the marbles that you like best!

Try this

Shine a flashlight into a marble. If it sparkles and reflects back at you, it probably has **aventurine** in it. Aventurine shines like gold or silver. But it's really tiny flecks of copper or steel. The Vitro company used to put it in their marbles.

Check the green and black cat's-eyes first! How can you find a Vitro cat's-eye? The ribbons through the middle are very wavy. Japanese cat's-eyes have straighter ones.

Chapter 7

Marble Trivia

- In wartime, soldiers played marbles. It was something to do when they were far from home. But marbles also became strange weapons for some soldiers!

  After World War I, the soldiers were promised extra pay. But they didn't get their money. Some were very angry.

  They went to Washington, D.C. They protested. Policemen came on horses to control them. The policemen had guns. The soldiers only had marbles.

They threw the marbles on the street.
The marbles went under the horses' feet.
Many animals slipped and fell. Horses
and riders were hurt.

This became known as The Battle of
Anacostia Flats. But the veterans still
didn't get their bonuses.

In 1932, the soldiers protested again.
They wanted their money. They were
asked to wait until 1945 to get paid. But
times were tough. The Great Depression
was going on. And they were poor. The
veterans needed the money to live. They
threw marbles again.

More than 100 people died in these
battles.

- The first **glassies** were really glass bottle stoppers. Glass stoppers were used before metal bottle caps. Children used them as marbles!

- In Germany, marbles were called **clickers** by store owners.

- Women wore marbles in Germany in the late 1800s! How? They wore hats and hatpins in those days. And guess what was at the end of the hatpin? It was a pretty stone marble!

- Some presidents played marbles in their free time. History says that Lincoln was a very fine marble player. Washington, Jefferson, and Adams also played the game.

- In the late 1700s and early 1800s, captains of sailing ships used marbles. But they didn't play games with them! They used marbles for two things. They were used to keep their ships on course and to make money. Usually sandbags were used in the bottom of ships to keep them upright in the water. But some captains used bags of marbles instead! Then at the end of the trip, they sold the marbles. That's how German marbles got to the West Indies.

- The term **blackball** comes from marbles. Long ago, black and white marbles were used for voting. Sometimes clubs used marbles to vote on new members.

 To vote, a person chose either a black or white marble. It was hidden in the hand. Then the marble was dropped into a small wooden box. A white marble meant "Yes." A black marble meant "No."

After everyone voted, the box was opened. More black balls in the box meant a person was not chosen. That person was *blackballed.*

- In 1893, you could buy 1,000 china marbles for 35¢, 12 **sulphides** for 25¢, or 100 red agates for $3.00. Today, a single sulphide might cost $100.00!

Just for Fun—Think About It

- Many marble hunters search near old schools or parks. Children played with marbles in those places. And sometimes they lost marbles in the dirt or grass.

- Marble hunters also search near old glass factories. Some glass factories made marbles to sell. So old marbles might be buried near the buildings.

  Often factory workers made marbles for fun. They made marbles for their children from glass left over from their jobs.

- 10,000 marbles weigh 100 pounds. This was called a **hundredweight.** Catalogs like Sears Roebuck and Montgomery Ward sold 10-pound bags of marbles. You do the math. How many marbles did a child get if she or he bought one bag?

  What would you do with this many marbles?

(See page 56 for the answer.)

- Now hold out your hands. Close your eyes. Hold one stone marble and one glass marble. How can you tell them apart? The stone marble will feel colder to the touch!
- Some children played marble games with nuts or fruit pits. Others played with the knucklebones of sheep. Look around your home or yard. What "marbles" can you find?
- **Riddle:** What do you get if you put these things together into a bag? A bumblebee. A wasp. A boy scout. A hurricane. A light bulb. A corkscrew. And a grasshopper.

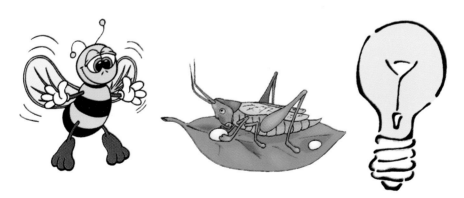

(See page 56 for the answer.)

- Here are some new names for old marbles. Can you guess what colors they are?
  1. ketchup and mustard
  2. Christmas tree
  3. zebra
  4. blue zebra
  5. cub scout
  6. bumblebee
  7. superman
  8. liberty

(See page 56 for the answer.)

Glossary

The Glossary includes words from *Marvelous Marbles.* There are also other words and phrases that marble players use.

accessories things to go with marbles

aggies marbles made from agate

aventurine shiny copper pieces added to some marbles

Benningtons brown and blue marbles made from pottery

blackball means of voting using black and white marbles

bowl to roll a marble along the ground or floor

bumboozer another name for a shooter in street games

cat's-eye glass marble made in Japan; clear glass with a band of color in the middle

clickers what marbles were called in Germany

commies common, "everyday" clay marbles

end-of-day marble valuable marble made at the end of the factory work day; it is different from others

fudging cheating by putting hand over the ring before shooting

game marbles usually 5/8 inch in size; used in most marble games

glassies	glass bottle stoppers used as marbles
glaze	painted on marbles to make them shiny
hundredweight	measurement based on 10,000 marbles weighing 100 pounds
lagging	how to choose who goes first in a marble game
marrididdles	homemade clay marbles
mibs	same as commies
pee wees	small marbles (1/2 inch or less)
pitching line	line from where a player shoots a marble

playing for fair	all marbles are returned to their owners after the game is over
playing for keeps	winner gets to keep all the marbles collected in the game
porcelain	material that some dishes are made from
scrumpy knuckle	knuckles off the ground when shooting
semiprecious stones	not as valuable as precious stones like diamonds
shooter	the most important marble in marble games

snooger   barely missed shot

steelies   hollow steel marbles

sulphides   clearies with tiny clay figures inside

taws   same as shooters

to stick   the shooter stays inside the ring

Answers

page 49   There were 1,000 marbles in a single bag!

page 50   A collection of machine-made marbles!

page 51   1. red and yellow; 2. green and red; 3. white with black stripes; 4. white with dark blue strips; 5. yellow and white; 6. yellow and black; 7. blue with red and yellow stripes; 8. white with blue and red